The Spaghetti and Meatball Adventure

By Louise Bello

Illustrated by Pompea Imondi

The Spaghetti and Meatball Adventure

Copyright © 2020 Louise Bello

Produced and printed
by Stillwater River Publications.
All rights reserved. Written and produced in the
United States of America. This book may not be reproduced
or sold in any form without the expressed, written
permission of the author and publisher.

Visit our website at
www.StillwaterPress.com
for more information.

First Stillwater River Publications Edition

Library of Congress Control Number: 2020911240

ISBN: 978-1-952521-24-9

1 2 3 4 5 6 7 8 9 10

Written by Louise Bello
Illustrated by Pompea Imondi
Published by Stillwater River Publications,
Pawtucket, RI, USA.

*The views and opinions expressed
in this book are solely those of the author
and do not necessarily reflect the views
and opinions of the publisher.*

*This book is dedicated to my grandchildren,
James Joseph Black III (Trey) and Vienna Stone Bello.*

*You are the loves of my life,
and fill my heart with hope every day.*

Nona sat at her kitchen table and looked out the window thinking, "Oh, how I wish I was not so old. I would so like to gather together the ingredients for spaghetti and meatballs. And then I would let the gravy simmer all day on the stove so the house would smell like home. And I would invite my wonderful family over for a feast. But I am too tired. I guess I will retire to my bed and pray for dreams of family and good times gone by."

Little did Nona know that a very interesting and tasty adventure was about to happen.

Sophia Spaghetti sat on her cupboard shelf feeling bored. Sophia wanted adventure. She knew that Tito Tomato Sauce was on the shelf below her, and she knew that he would be ready for an adventure, too.

Tito Tomato Sauce felt sad and lonely. He wished that he could get out of the cupboard and explore the world.

"Sophia, you seem a bit out of sorts today. What is bothering you?" asked Benito Bread Crumbs.

Sophia sadly replied, "Oh Benito, I am so bored. When I was made three months ago in the spaghetti factory in San Marino, Italy, and then shipped to the North End of Boston in America, I really thought I would be doing exciting things. I thought I would be meeting wonderful gravy friends who would simmer together for hours and make homes smell so good. And then we would be served to people who appreciate delicious food."

"I know what you mean. I come from a very popular family of bread crumbs. We are used in only the finest restaurants of southern Italy. I have been sitting here so long I am probably stale now," Benito replied.

"We need to do something about this. We need to somehow get in touch with Tito Tomato Sauce. He lives on the shelf below us. Orazia Olive Oil lives there, too. They will know what to do." Sophia said.

"Follow me Benito I am going to push the door open so Tito can hear us." She wiggled forward and pushed, and the cupboard door swung open.

Susana Salt and Placido Pepper, who were sitting behind Sophia, were taking a nap. But they woke up when the door opened.

"Hi guys! We are going on an adventure. Come with us!" Sophia insisted.

Susana Salt and Placido Pepper rubbed their eyes, looked at one another, shrugged, and then said, "Sure!"

On the shelf below, Tito Tomato Sauce was in a deep conversation with Orazia Olive Oil when the door flew open.

"Oh my goodness! From our mouths to God's ears, Tito." Orazia screeched.

"I know, Orazia. We were just talking about busting out of this place and having some fun. Amazing! Just amazing!" said Tito Tomato Sauce. "Now how do we get out of here?" Tito asked, looking puzzled.

"Tito! Tito! Look up here! It's me, Sophia Spaghetti!"

"Oh my goodness, Sophia. I thought I would never see you again," replied Tito with tears in his eyes.

"We have not been on an adventure in a long time. Let's get everybody together and have some fun. I have Benito Bread Crumbs, Susana Salt, and Placido Pepper with me. Who is down there with you?" Sophia Spaghetti asked.

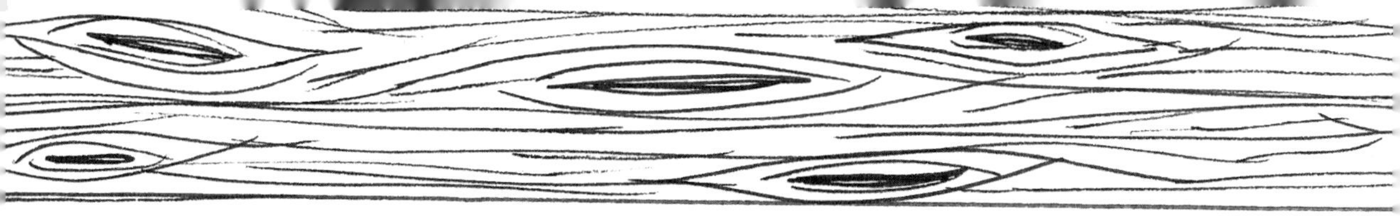

"Orazia Olive Oil, Pia Parsley, and Bacchus Bay Leaf." Tito answered.

"Let's jump down so we can all meet together on the counter," Sophia said.

Orazia, Pia, Bacchus, and Tito braced themselves together and jumped. Obasi Onion and Gaetano Garlic were in a wire mesh bin hanging next to the counter. On the way down, Bacchus Bay Leaf bumped into the bin, tipping it just enough for Obasi and Gaetano to tumble down onto the counter with them. Everyone landed safely.

Now it was Sophia Spaghetti, Benito Bread Crumbs, Susana Salt, and Placido Pepper's turn to jump. Susana Salt started to cry. She was excited, but a little afraid.

"Don't worry Susana," Sophia said, "you and Placido can stand between Benito and me when we jump and we will help brace your fall."

Once Susana was ready, they stood side by side. "Okay, push together really hard and jump," Sophia said. They all pushed themselves together and waddled their way to the edge of the shelf.

Tito Tomato Sauce had dragged Mario and Marcello Moppines up from the rack next to the counter and laid them out for their friends to land on. Benito counted, "One...two... three... jump!" And they did. They all fell and landed in a comfortable pile on the soft moppine towels.

As they all pulled themselves together on the counter, they heard a sweet little voice say, "Oh my goodness what is happening?" They turned and saw Sabrina Sugar. Sophia explained what they were doing, and Sabrina happily joined them.

"We need Bianka Bowl, Santino Spoon, and Congi Colander to come down from the cupboard above, too" said Tito.

"I have an idea." Sabrina answered. "Well as you all know, Bianka Bowl is getting old and cannot get around the way she used to. We have to be very careful." They listened carefully to Sabrina's directions.

They all worked together. Benito grabbed Mario Moppine and tied him to the cupboard door handle.

Then he jumped down and helped Bacchus Bay Leaf and Gaetano Garlic climb on top of Tito. They pulled the cupboard door open, and then held up Mario Moppine as Santino Spoon gently pushed Bianka Bowl and Congi Colander onto Mario. Then he jumped into Bianka Bowl. They gently lowered her to the counter.

The noise they made woke Nona. Nona slowly got out of bed and walked down the hallway into the kitchen to see what the commotion was all about.

The ingredients heard her coming and froze still on the counter. When Nona came around the corner into the kitchen, she saw them and said to herself, "How did all these ingredients get here? I must have taken them out to make spaghetti and meatballs but then got too tired and went to bed."

"Oh Mama Mia! I can't remember anything anymore. Well, I will take the rest of the ingredients out and get the pans ready. Maybe I will have enough energy in the morning to put together a nice meal for my family."

Nona took out a boiling pan for the spaghetti and a simmering pan for the gravy and placed them on the stove.

She looked down at the counter and took an inventory of the ingredients that were there. Then she walked to the cupboard and noticed the moppine tied to the handle. "How in heaven's name did this get here? I really am getting strange and forgetful in my old age!"

She untied the moppine and placed it on the counter. "Now what else do I need?" Nona asked herself. "Ah yes... parsley, parmesan cheese, beef, and eggs."

Nona opened the refrigerator and placed the parsley, cheese, beef, and an egg inside on a moppine. "Now I have everything I need to make spaghetti and meatballs."

Nona slowly walked back down the hallway and went back to bed.

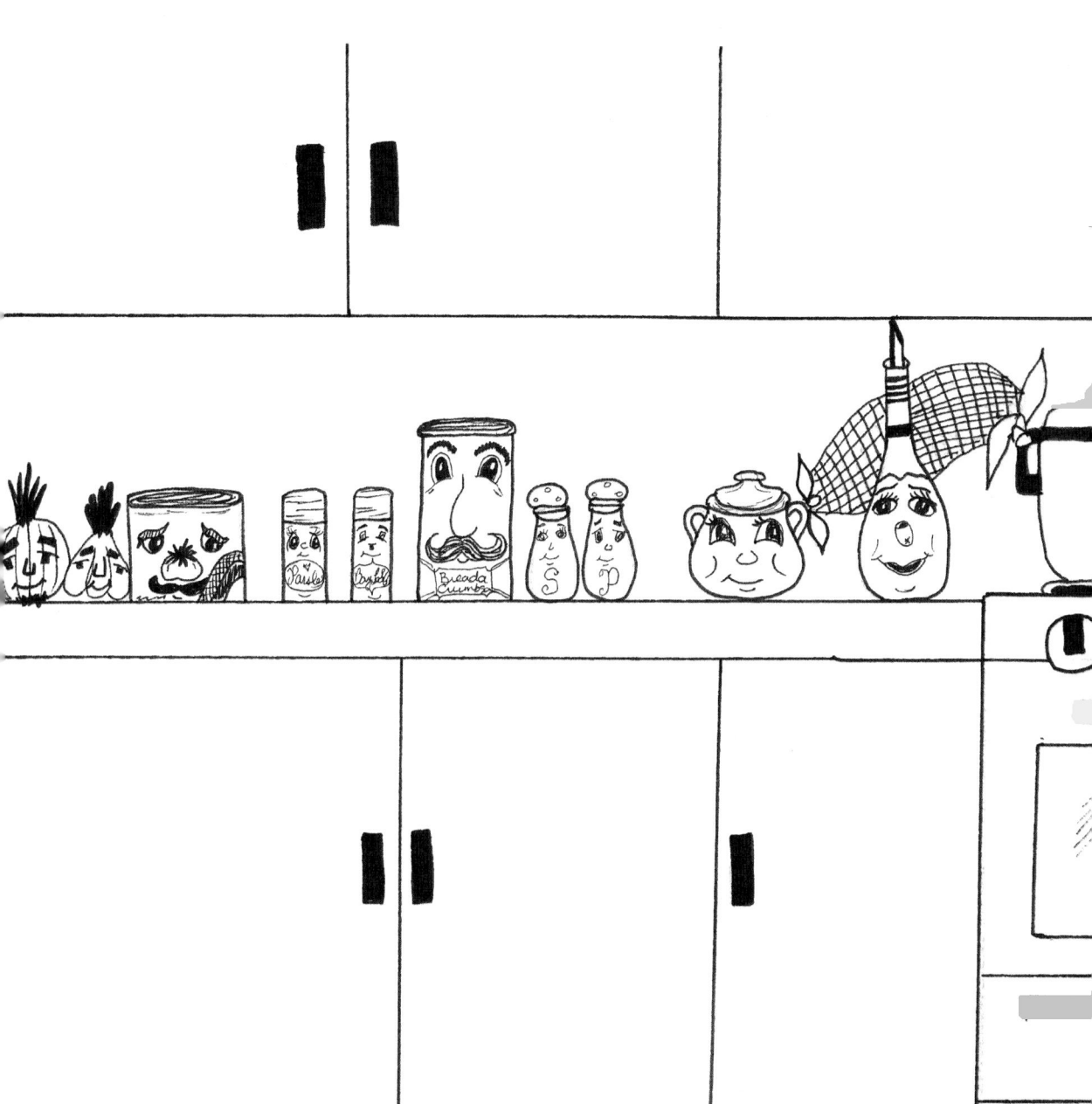

When Sophia heard the bedroom door close, she said, "Wow! That was a close one. We all have to be more quiet."

"We have to get water into Pablo Pan so that Sophia can dance and soften later," said Orazia Olive Oil. The ingredients formed a long line and tied one end of Marcello Moppine to the counter and the other end to the stove. Then they grabbed the water hose from the sink to spray water into Pablo.

"Now we have to get Pia Parsley, Benedito Beef, Paolina Parmesan, and Elenora Egg out of the refrigerator." Stefano Stove quietly squeaked his oven door open. First, Marcello Moppine jumped and arranged himself on the oven door. Then Bacchus Bay Leaf and Gaetano Garlic jumped together. Bacchus and Gaetano stepped to the side so that Sophia Spaghetti, Benito Bread Crumbs, and Tito Tomato Sauce could jump down, too.

Gaetano and Bacchus grabbed Marcello and slipped him in the handle of Rita Refrigerator, pulled her open, then jumped onto the middle shelf.

Sophia Spaghetti climbed on top of Benito Bread Crumbs as Tito Tomato Sauce pushed his weight against Benito to support them. Sophia slowly leaned against the middle shelf of Rita. Gaetano and Bacchus gently helped Pia, Benedito, Paolina, and Elenora slide down Sophia. They were able, one at a time, to work up enough speed when sliding down Sophia to bounce onto Benito, and then onto Tito, and then hop up.

When they were done, everyone was safely on the counter.

"Okay everyone let's get to work," said Sophia Spaghetti. Sabatino Simmering Pot was ready and waiting on Stefano Stove. Orazia Olive Oil moved to the edge of the counter and gently spilled a little oil into Sabatino.

Next, Gaetano Garlic, Pia Parsley, and Bacchus Bay Leaf jumped from the counter into Sabatino. They simmered for a bit while Sophia helped Tito remove his cover. They stood on the counter looking at each other.

"Tito, this has been a wonderful adventure. I am so happy we were able to do it together. I will meet you on the table in a little while," Sophia said.

Tito and Sophia hugged, then Sophia hoisted Tito up and poured him into Sabatino. Suzana Salt poured some of herself into the boiling water in Pablo Pan. The water started to boil! The gravy was cooking!

Bianka Bowl stood proud on the counter as Benedito Beef, Benito Bread Crumbs, Paolina Parmesan, Elenora Egg, and Obasi Onion climbed in. All the ingredients mixed together and rolled themselves into medium size meatballs. Stanley Sheet who lives on the counter, laid himself flat and the meatballs rolled out of Bianka Bowl onto Stanley Sheet.

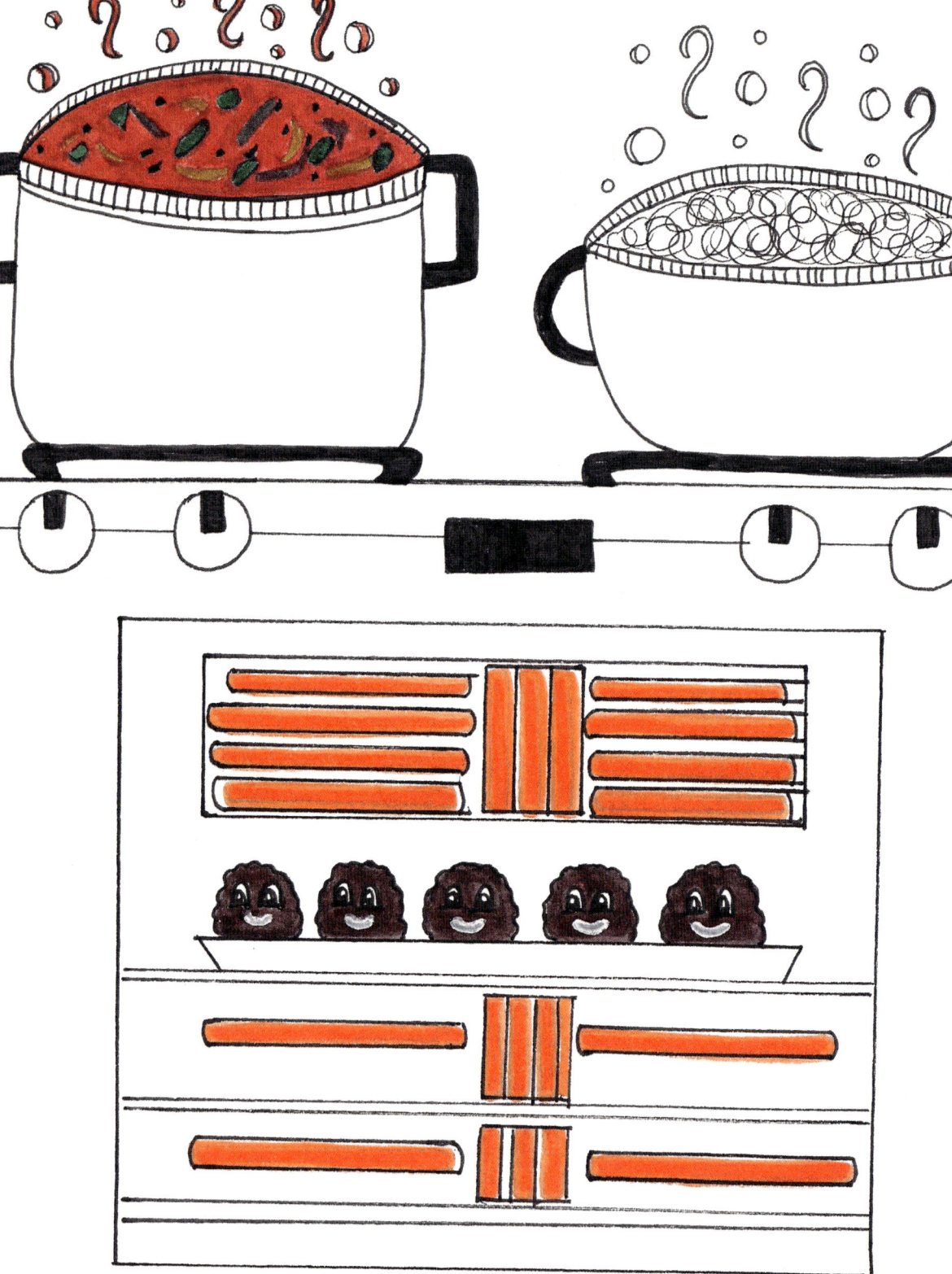

Marcello and Mario tied themselves together, then Sophia tied one end of them to the drawer handle below the counter. Stefano Stove opened his oven door as Marcello and Mario slipped around Stefano's door handle. Stanley was able to slide right down and into Stefano Stove. The meatballs began to cook.

Nona woke to a wonderful smell. She walked to the kitchen and saw the gravy simmering on the stove and the water slowly boiling for spaghetti. She carefully lifted the lid off of the gravy and took a deep breath.

"Oh that smells wonderful, but where are the meatballs?" She grabbed the moppines on the counter and opened the oven door. "They look good!" she exclaimed.

Nona placed the meatballs into the gravy. She turned and saw all the other ingredients on the counter and said, "Oh, I must have forgotten to clean these up. I will do it later. Right now I am going to call my family and tell them to come over for dinner."

Nona walked back to the living room to make the call. She decided to call her daughter first who would tell the rest of the family. When her daughter answered the phone, Nona said, "the meatballs and gravy are simmering and I have the water in the pan for the spaghetti. All you have to do is bring some good Italian bread. Tell everyone to come over to eat dinner"

Her daughter said, "Okay, Mom."

Nona then set the table and cleaned up the kitchen. She quickly became tired, so she went and rested in her chair. She slept so soundly she did not hear her family come through the back door into the kitchen. Her daughter walked down to the living room and saw her asleep in her chair. She went back to the kitchen and told her family. "Let's whisper. Nona is asleep."

Nona's family then boiled Sophia Spaghetti, finished setting the table, cut up the Italian bread on the bread board, and put everything out on the table.

Nona woke up and looked at the time and said, "Oh no! My family will be here any minute! There is no way I will get dinner cooked in time!"

She got up out of her chair and walked down the hall to the kitchen. The wonderful smells floating through the air had such a heavenly scent. As she turned the corner into the kitchen, she saw her family.

"Oh! What a surprise!" Nona said.

"Let's sit and have some spaghetti and meatballs, Mom," her daughter said.

"Good idea!" said Nona.

All the ingredients had blended together to create a delicious delectable taste. The meatballs seemed to be smiling and Sophia Spaghetti was al dente and curled all around in the gravy. The ingredients were happy!

Nona's family sat down at the table and talked while sharing the spaghetti, meatballs and sliced Italian bread. Everyone was happy! Nona did not feel so old anymore. She looked around at her family and took a deep breath to enjoy all the wonderful smells.

All Nona could do was smile.

About the Author

Louise Bello has been an elementary educator for over 21 years. She is a literacy coach for Providence College, an Orton Gillingham Dyslexia Tutor for the Children's Dyslexia Center of Rhode Island, and an inspiration to her students, families, and fellow educators. Louise wrote *The Spaghetti and Meatball Adventure* to show children that working together can be an adventure, and make dreams come true. She lives that belief every day, partnering with colleagues and community members to help others through various charitable works. Louise lives in North Providence, Rhode Island. She enjoys all types of creative expression, especially writing and painting. She is a wife, mother, and grandmother, and plans to use writing to spread her message of kindness, unity, and family.

About the Illustrator

Pompea Uriati Imondi has been an early childhood educator for over 15 years. She is the mother of two wonderful children, and enjoys learning through their eyes, and uses their point of view to drive her teaching. She has illustrated several published works, such as *The Magic Ceiling, Friends Forever, The Dragon of Many Colors,* and *The Blue Kataroo*. Pompea hopes to reach children of all ages and inspire creativity and personal growth through her artwork.

Made in the USA
Columbia, SC
31 July 2020